Read and Rhyme
LEVEL 1 ★

Wick to Chick

by Anita Stasson

Consultant:
Beth Gambro
Reading Specialist
Yorkville, Illinois

Contents

BEARPORT
PUBLISHING

Minneapolis, Minnesota

Wick to Chick

I see a lit **wick**.

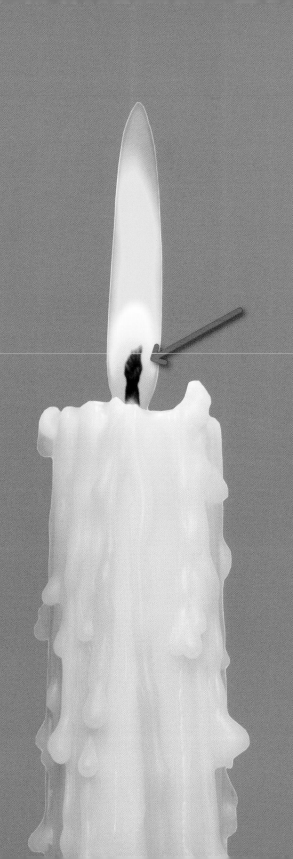

I see a small **tick**.

I see a red **brick**.

I see a wood **stick**.

I see a big **kick**.

I see a magic **trick**.

I see a yellow **chick**.

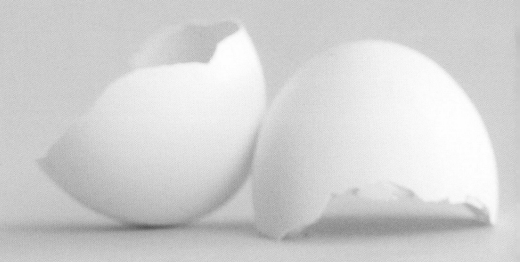

Key Words in the -ick Family

brick

chick

kick

stick

tick

trick

wick

Other **-ick** Words: **lick, pick, sick**

Index

About the Author

Anita Stasson lives in Minnesota. She thinks rhyming is the bee's knees.

Teaching Tips

Before Reading

- ✔ Introduce rhyming words and the **–ick** word family to readers.
- ✔ Guide readers on a picture walk through the text by asking them to name the things shown.
- ✔ Discuss book structure by showing children where text will appear consistently on pages. Highlight the supportive pattern of the book.

During Reading

- ✔ Encourage readers to read with their finger and point to each word as it is read. Stop periodically to ask children to point to a specific word in the text.
- ✔ When encountering unknown words, prompt readers with encouraging cues such as:
  - **Does that word look like a word you already know?**
  - **Does it rhyme with another word you have already read?**

After Reading

- ✔ Write the key words on index cards.
  - **Have readers match them to pictures in the book.**
- ✔ Ask readers to identify their favorite page in the book. Have them read that page aloud.
- ✔ Choose an **–ick** word. Ask children to pick a word that rhymes with it.
- ✔ Ask children to create their own rhymes using **–ick** words. Encourage them to use the same pattern found in the book.

Credits: Cover, © Africa Studio/Shutterstock and © Avalon_Studio/iStock; 2–3, © Rtimages/iStock; 4–5, © Risto0/iStock; 6–7, © Akintevs/Shutterstock; 8–9, © Alexan2008/iStock; 10–11, © Serhii Bobyk/Shutterstock; 12–13, © aluxum/iStock; 14–15, © Pixel-Shot/Shutterstock; 16T (L to R), © Akintevs/Shutterstock, © Pixel-Shot/Shutterstock, © Serhii Bobyk/ Shutterstock, and © Alexan2008/iStock; and 16B (L to R), © Risto0/iStock, © aluxum/iStock, and © Rtimages/iStock.

Bearport Publishing Company Product Development Team
President: Jen Jenson; Director of Product Development: Spencer Brinker; Managing Editor: Allison Juda; Associate Editor: Naomi Reich; Senior Designer: Colin O'Dea; Associate Designer: Elena Klinkner; Associate Designer: Kayla Eggert; Product Development Specialist: Anita Stasson

Library of Congress Cataloging-in-Publication Data is available at www.loc.gov or upon request from the publisher.
ISBN: 979-8-88822-049-8 (hardcover); ISBN: 979-8-88822-243-0 (paperback); ISBN: 979-8-88822-364-2 (ebook)